Computer

Fundamentals

For Adults

ISBN-10: 1484965175

ISBN-13: 978-1484965177

THE CASE & COMPONENTS
Book: 1 of 10
By: David Babb

Introduction

The most common factor with, computer software, hardware and network issues is, that there are a considerable amount of users which do not know or have not had the opportunity to learn the basics about their devices or networks.

In most cases we either rely on the computer manufacturer, software manufacturer or someone we know to assist us in the setup and operation of your devices and software.

In the end, you are assisted in getting started with your computer but then it has been left up to you to discover or learn about the features and options you have with your device. What happens when something does not work right? This has prompted me to create a very easy to understand educational tool at an extremely economical price including pictures on each topic for visual association of what the components look like and an explanation of what their basic functions are.

There are pictures for each to topic which makes it easy for you to visually associate.

There are no technical terms in here.

Created for the: novice or beginner.

David Babb

Chapter 1

Cases & Components

Cases come in many shapes and sizes for many different reasons.

If you bought your computer at a local general retailer you may have gotten a great price on the purchase of your new machine.

In the beginning it may have run really great but what did you really get inside?

This great priced computer has to give up something in order for you to get it at the price you paid for it.

In the end result "you get what you pay for".

Upgradability - Storage Size – Memory - Processor Speed or the lack thereof on any of these components.

Another words the price was great but in most cases the system will start having problems after a few years.

Case Function

The case performs many functions and also holds most of the hardware that is the make-up of what you know to be your computer.

The case is responsible to contain your hardware components and to keep everything inside cool or at least at a good operating temperature and also minimizes noise.

Most of these components generate heat and need to be cooled so they do not overheat and cease to function.

Common Tower Sizes:

Small Form Factor Case

A small form factor (SFF) is a computer case designed to minimize the volume of a desktop computer. For comparison purposes, the size of an SFF case is usually measured in liters. SFFs are available in a variety of sizes and shapes, including shoeboxes, cubes, and book-sized PCs. Their smaller and often lighter construction has made them popular as Home Theater PCs and as Gaming Computers.

Mini-Size Tower

These cases are slightly bigger than the desktop cases and usually have 3 internal drive bays.

Expandability is again a problem with these cases.

Mini-cases normally stand at a height of 12-18 inches.

These cases are bigger than mini-towers and in fact, mid-tower cases are the most widely used computer cases worldwide.

They usually contain 4 internal drive ways and a similar number of external bays.

These cases can be easily expanded or upgraded to higher versions depending on the need and requirement.

These cases are ideally suitable for any type of computer irrespective of whether it is a simple, business, or any advanced system.

The normal height of a mid-size tower is 24inches.

Full Size Tower

These cases are commonly employed in the design of servers, mainframes, and advanced workstations that can handle multiple applications.
The number of internal drive bays inside these cases can be anywhere between 6 and 10. Drive bays are where you can

add more hard drives or CD-ROM's. These cases contain a similar number of externally accessible drive bays.

Additionally, a great amount of space is present inside these cases and can be used for placing any number of hard drives, CD ROMs, and PCI cards.

Full-sized cases are generally huge with a height that is equal to or more than 30 inches.

Insulated Cases

The black foam-like material "absorbs sound" from inside the case, making the noise produce outside of the case quieter. These cases do have their downsides.

For noise insulation to work properly, you need to have the case as sealed as possible, which can seriously affect thermal performance if there isn't sufficient airflow from the fans.

It is very difficult to keep a computer extremely cool and quiet. It is usually one or the other without getting water cooling involved, which we will not be covering.

Water Cooling is not something a novice should be doing. As we all know water and electric do not mix.

Air Flow:

Positive Airflow:

The "Front Fan" pulls the cool air in through the front of the case over the components and pushes the hot air out of the vents in the rear of the case.

Negative Airflow:

A "Rear Fan" pulls the cool air in from the front case vents over the internal components and out of the back of the case.

Equalized Airflow:

The "Fans Front and Rear" are pulling air from the vents in the front of the case.

This creates a constant wind- tunnel effect inside the case if one fans does fail the other will continue to function until you replace the failed unit.

This is kind of a built-on fail safe, but don't rely in it as your cooling capacity has just been cut in half.

Chapter 2

PSU – Power Supply& Connections

The power supply provides the component's in the computer with power. Pushing the power button to turn on your computer many components start up at once. Hard-Drives in particular can use as much as four times the power to startup.

Many of these components use far more power to start up than when they are running.
Most power supplies have extra capacity built-in to handle this power demand for short periods of time.
The standard power supply is usually cheaper and a lot more common.
In this type of PSU, all of the cables are hard-wired into the unit.

While this is cheaper and provides slightly better performance, you are stuck with extra cables that you do not use.
This makes cable routing; messy and can affect air flow within the case.

MODULAR POWER SUPPLY

Modular Power Supplies have detachable cables.
This means you only use the cables you need.
This makes routing and storage, much easier, looks much
neater and is less restrictive to the air flow.

PSU CONNECTORS:

20 PIN PLUS 4, CONNECTOR

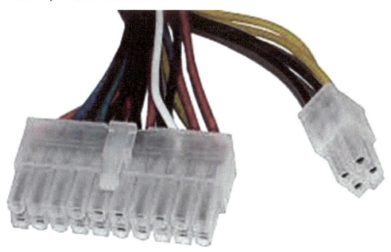

This connector provides power to the motherboard itself and to the expansion cards also.

The 4-pins shown are not required on some motherboards.

Molex Connector - Male and Female

This is one of the standard connectors from your power supply.

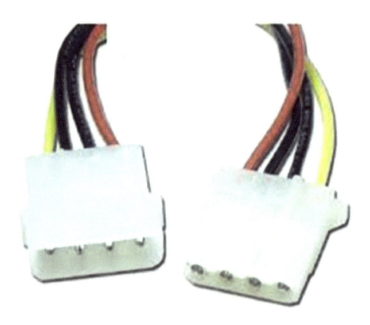

Supplies power to hard drive and is also considered to be a wild card type of connector. Provides power to the floppy drive which is obsolete and now it is used to primarily power card-readers.

Floppy Drive Connector

Provides power to the floppy drive which are-not used today. Now it is used to primarily power Card-readers.

Compare Molex to Floppy

Sata Connector

This connector is used for the, Sata hard drives.

You will not find this on the Older Power Supplies.

4 + 4 PIN CPU POWER

This 4-Pin connector provides power to the CPU or Central processing Unit with all of the power it needs.
It is usually located on the motherboard next to the CPU.

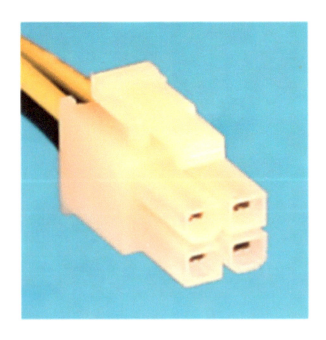

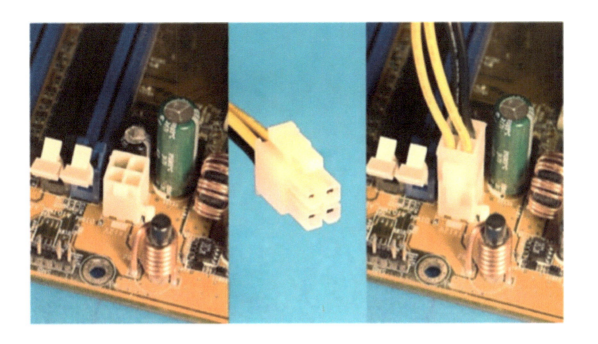

CPIE 6+2 CONNECTOR

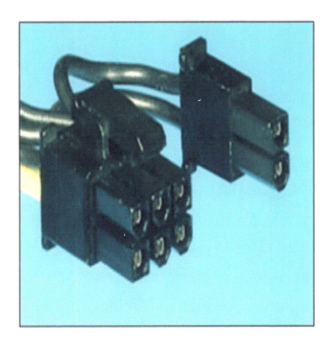

This connector provides power for the more recent Graphics Cards.
The most common is 2 six pin connectors but some cards require an 8 Pin Connector. That is why the 6+2 pin connector

Fire Wire

FireWire quickly became popular on audio and video devices like digital camcorders. The reason for this popularity was the speed; the original FireWire 400 standard could achieve a data transfer rate of up to 400 Mbit/s. USB with only able to manage a maximum data transfer rate of 12 Mbit/s. The massive gap in capability made FireWire an obvious choice for anyone with the need to move big files.

Chapter3

MOTHER BOARDS BASICS

This is the most obvious, component inside your computer.
All components communicate thru the motherboard whether
it is by slotting into it directly or thru cables.
All parts communicate thru the motherboard.

Motherboards are commonly split into 2 groups, those for
AMD Processors and those for Intel Processors.
They are almost identical except for the socket on the
motherboard which they plug into.
The pins on the CPU must match the socket they plug into.

Motherboards are divided into three basic sizes.
The ATX is the larger of the 2 most common sizes and offers
the most upgradability, this board usually offers 4 to 6
expansion slots and often has more Sata and IDE Ports,
including some have the ability to have more than one
graphics card usually for gaming.

This is the area you will see on the back of your case.

Micro-ATX

This motherboard is more common for less powerful machines such as you would find in an office or in a budget PC from Dell or HP.

They offer great balance between power and size and usually provide 2 to 4 expansion slots unlike the main ATX board offering: 4 to 6.

Some people prefer the full size ATX as there is more room and it is not so cramped even though they do not use more than what the Micro-ATX offers.

Mini-ATX Motherboard

These have become very popular within the last couple of years with the introduction of net ops which is the desktop equivalent of net books.

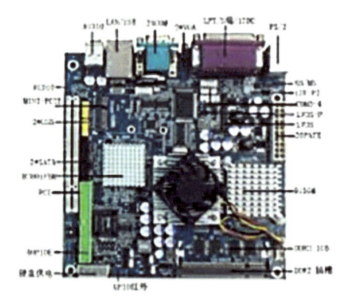

The reasoning for this Mini ATX is simple, very small, low power for basic tasks, which is what we use a computer for 90% of the time. The processor is integrated into the motherboard.

It is the least flexible and upgradable compared to the other most common types of motherboards.

Mini ITX Motherboard

Mini ITX boards have proved over the past few years.
Mini ITX motherboards now sport many of the same features as full size ATX boards.
Mini-ITX boards have low power consumption, which makes them useful for home theater PC systems, where fan noise can detract from the cinema experience.

CHIPSET MANUFACTURERS

There are many different companies that manufacture motherboards the chipsets themselves are always manufactured by the CPU Manufacturer.
AMD makes the CPU for their motherboards and Intel makes the CPU for their motherboards.

Intel retains its grip on the chipset market ensuring you'll pretty much only see motherboards based on its chipsets and therefore its design blueprints.

The exception is that Nvida makes CPU's for both Intel and AMD which is geared more for the gamer.

Companies like SIS and VIA used to make the CPU's for both CPU processor types but are not really considered to be in the mainstream desktop market for quite some time now.

NORTHBRIDGE CHIP

The Northbridge Chipset allows the; CPU, Ram and Graphics Cards to Communicate with each other as well as connecting to the Southbridge Chipset.

The Northbridge Chipset is also referred to as the "Memory Controller Hub" in the Intel systems.

On newer systems (such as those based on i3 and i5 processors) the Northbridge no longer exists as a chip on the motherboard.

The PCIExpress and the RAM Controllers have been incorporated into the CPU.

This has the advantage of reducing latency between the processor and memory which means it does not take as long for the processor and the memory to communicate with each other.

In motherboards with integrated graphics "video card is not used" the graphics chip is usually incorporated within the Northbridge.

In the cheaper motherboards this is done by taking up PCIE lanes which means any graphic card added after wards would generally not perform well.

SOUTHBRIDGE CHIP

The Southbridge Chipset is responsible for the communication between the other components; External Devices, Audio and the Networking with the Northbridge.

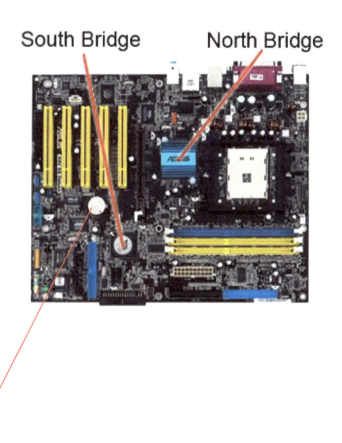

CMOS & BATTERY

CMOS is used as a form of nonvolatile memory. It needs power supplied to it in order to maintain the data that is stored in it.
The CMOS battery is that power source.

MOTHERBOARD FLOW CHART

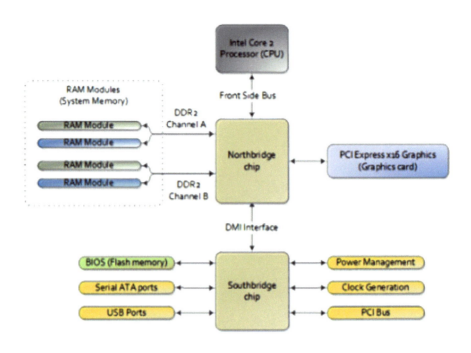

Chapter 4

CPU Chips and Sockets

The Processor Socket on the motherboard.
All modern CPU sockets use some form of lever to lock the processor down against the motherboard.
This ensures that there is a good connection between the pins and contacts of the motherboard and processor.

AMD SOCKET AM3

INTEL SOCKET775

INTEL SOCKET1366

CPU PROCESSOR

Central Processing Unit

The CPU (Central Processing Unit) or processor is the brain of the computer – it's where all calculations are carried out. Short of gaming, pretty much all the work a computer does is carried out by the CPU; while RAM and hard drives are important, they simply act as storage while data manipulation is carried out by the processor.
The most powerful consumer CPU's currently the same processor held in the hand "below" for a size reference.

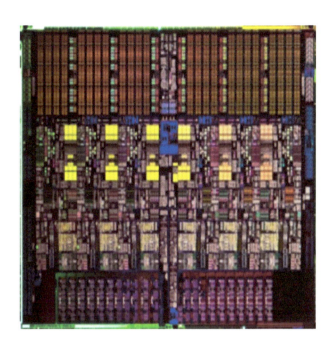

CPU Clock Speed

One of the most common things you'll see when looking at CPU specifications is the processor's clock speed, measured in gigahertz (GHz), with 1GHz being equal to 1 billion hertz or cycles per second.

This means that a 1GHz processor is able to carry out 1 billion calculations every second.

As a general rule of thumb a processor with a higher clock speed is more powerful than one with a lower clock speed. However this isn't the whole story, as different CPUs can do different amounts of work per cycle.

One way to understand this is to imagine two people trying to fill identical swimming pools from a well with nothing but buckets.

If both buckets were the same size, the faster person would be the one who can make more trips between the well and their swimming pool in the same time frame.

However, the slower person could fill their pool just as fast if they carry more water per-trip with a bigger bucket.

CPU Multiple Cores

When looking to buy a new computer, you'll be constantly barraged with mentions of cores – Dual cores! Quad cores! Hexa-Core! What does it actually mean?

Up until 2004, all processors had just one core, or processing unit. A processor was made faster by increasing that core's clock speed.

The disadvantage to this was that higher clock speeds generated much more heat, leading to massive, noisy heat-sinks.

It eventually reached the stage where it was simply infeasible to keep increasing the clock speed.

The solution was to create a processor with two cores – that is, a single processor with two smaller, lower speed processing units which can carry out different instructions. The benefit in this is obvious – why force a single unit to do lots of things at once when you can split the work between two slightly less capable units?

The first generations of dual core processors – the Intel Celeron D and AMD Athlon 64 X2 families, were not much more efficient than their single-cored predecessors. In fact, before the technology was perfected they generated more heat than ever.

However, over time they've become better and better; new computers have at least two cores, with single core CPUs used only for the absolutely cheapest computers (as well as for applications where lots of processing power simply isn't needed, such as net-books).

The performance gains do come down purely to clock speeds again. As an example, let's compare a 3.0GHz dual core processor with a 2.6GHz quad core processor.

This means that the dual core processor has 2 cores each running at 3.0GHz, giving the "equivalent" of a single core processor running at 6.0GHz.

Although each core on the quad core processor is running 400MHz slower, there are four cores – 4 cores each running at 2.6GHz gives the "equivalent" of 10.4GHz.

So logically, all quad core processors must be better than Dual Core processors, and all Hexa-core processors must be better than quads?

Well, it's not quite as simple as that, because it depends on what you want to do with the computer.

Most of the time computers are now used to doing lots of different things at once; opening a lot of tabs in a web browser, word processing, listening to music and instant messaging all at the same time.

This is where multi-core processors really perform, as they are able to split up the tasks and distribute them between the cores; the more cores you have, the more your CPU can handle at once.

However, there are some single tasks which require lots of processing power – editing video, working with large images in Photoshop or playing games.

Up until very recently most computer applications haven't been designed to make proper use of multiple cores. In this case, a processor with fewer cores at higher clock speeds will perform better.

CPU Cache

When performing some research on different CPUs, you may find cache, measured in kilobytes (KB) or megabytes (MB). This is a place where the most frequently used data is stored so that it is quickly accessible by the processor.
CPUs typically have at least 2 levels of cache (L1 and L2), with newer and more powerful ones having a third level (L3).
L1 is the fastest but smallest level of cache, whereas the higher levels tend to have much higher quantities but are slower (although still faster than accessing the data from the RAM).

CPU <u>AMD</u> & <u>INTEL</u>

Intel's instead decided to make a clean break with its new processors, introducing two new sockets (Socket 1156 and Socket 1366) and making backwards compatibility impossible.

However, Intel's most powerful processor is 25-50% faster than AMD's - the only downside is that it costs over three times as much!

To put it another way, for those looking to upgrade from an older AMD-based system, those looking for a good balance between price and performance and those who don't mind going without cutting edge technology, an AMD-based computer makes the most sense.

Where money is no object or performance is particularly important, an Intel-based system is probably better.

Of course, this is assuming you're looking into building your own computer.

If you just go to a store your mind will be made up for you; 80% of the time the computer will be built around an Intel CPU.

That's not a bad thing; you don't need to go hunting for an AMD computer necessarily.

Chapter5

CPU Cooling

With all the work that the CPU does, it generates a lot of heat. This heat has to go somewhere – if the CPU gets too hot, it will be damaged and won't work anymore. There are a lot of delicate electronics in there! This is where the CPU fan and heat-sink comes in. Just look for a big hunk of metal with a big fan on it. That will be the heat-sink!

The CPU is under that, and it's the only thing keeping your CPU from melting to your motherboard. If for some reason the CPU doesn't get cooled properly it'll shut itself off before any real damage can be caused. How does a heat-sink work?

The heat-sink uses levers or screws to keep the heat-sink pressed tightly against the CPU. A small amount of thermal paste between the two removes all the gaps. Heat is transferred from the surface of the CPU's heat spreader to the heat-sink via conduction. The heat spreads throughout the heat-sink out to the edges of the heat-sink, which are split into lots of thin fins. This increases the surface area of the heat-sink so when the fan on top blows down it pushes cooler air over the hot fins, taking heat away from the heat-sink.

Heat-Sinks Cooling

The only problem is that the stock cooler does not do the best job in the world.
Yes, it does keep the processor cool enough that it doesn't overheat, but it usually does not do it efficiently or quietly. The CPU heat-sink is often the noisiest part of the computer. There are many manufacturers who realize this is the case, so you'll find lots of companies which sell after-market CPU coolers.
These tend to be much bigger, providing many more fins and a much, much larger surface area for the heat to be transferred away from the heat-sink.

A bigger heat-sink also means that it can carry a larger fan which can spin slower to move the same amount of air, thus creating next noise.
To move the heat faster after-market coolers tend to use more heat pipes, which use liquids to transfer heat faster to the far ends of the heat-sink.

Compare that to the size of the stock AMD heat-sink, and you can see why it can keep a processor at room temperature while staying pretty much silent!

CPU Water Cooling

HOW IT WORKS!

Heat - the movement of energy from a hotter object to a cooler object-is never eliminated, but only moved elsewhere.

This is the role of all cooling systems.

To accomplish this, there are three primary modes of heat transfer.
Some forms of transfer can be duplicated using multiple methods (both natural and forced), but every cooling system uses these same basic processes:

Conduction - the transfer of heat through matter with no net displacement of the matter
Convection - the circulatory motion of a gas or liquid caused by the variation of its density and the action of gravity
Radiation - the process of transferring heat by emitting electromagnetic energy in the form of waves or particles

CPU Water COOLING

If you are just using your computer for average use then we would not recommend the expense or extra effort. The way your computer was bought, will work just fine.
If you are a serious gamer and over clock your CPU then this is going to almost certainly become a necessity.

Cooling Process

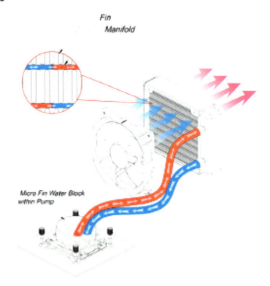

Fin

Manifold

Micro Fin Water Block
within Pump

Chapter 6

RAM Chips and Sockets

This is where the computer's memory is installed.
Most motherboards have two channels and either two or four slots (one or two for each channel).
 An exception is Intel's Socket 1366 chipset, which has three channels and six slots.

PRIMARY: DIMM_A1 & DIMM_ A2

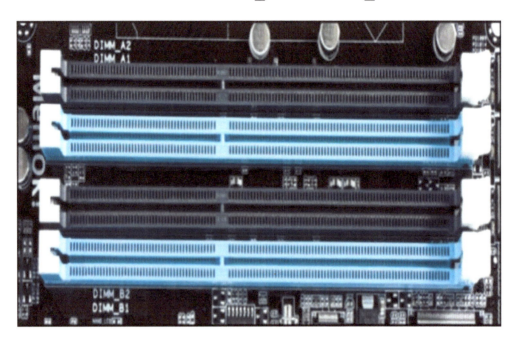

SECONDARY: DIMM_B1 & DIMM_B2

RAM CHIPS AND SOCKETS

In the picture above, it shows: DIMM_A1, DIMM_A2, DIMM_B1 and DIMM_B2.

This shows the order in which RAM should be inserted. The letter shows which channel the slot belongs to, while the number shows which slot is recognized first within the channel.

In this example, A1 must always be filled first – no RAM is recognized if this is not occupied.

After that, it is a little more flexible; you could choose to either fill the first channel by placing a second stick in A2, or use the second channel by placing it in B1.

It does not really matter either way, if you have identical sticks you can get a small performance boost by placing them in different channels (i.e. A1 and B1) as each stick is able to hold completely different memory and allows for greater multitasking.

RAM - RANDOM ACCESS MEMORY

The most common types of DIMMs are:

   168-pin DIMM, used for SDR SDRAM
   172-pin Micro-DIMM, used for DDR SDRAM
   184-pin DIMM, used for DDR SDRAM
   200-pin SO-DIMM, used for DDR SDRAM and DDR2 SDRAM
   204-pin SO-DIMM, used for DDR3 SDRAM
   214-pin Micro-DIMM, used for DDR2 SDRAM
   240-pin DIMM, used for DDR2 SDRAM, DDR3 SDRAM and FB-DIMM DRAM
   244-pin Mini-DIMM, used for DDR2 SDRAM

RAM SO-DIMM

SO-DIMM, or "small outline dual in-line memory module", is a type of computer memory built using integrated circuits. SO-DIMMs (also written SODIMMs) are a smaller alternative to a DIMM, being roughly half the size of regular DIMMs. SO-DIMMs are often used in systems that have limited space, such as notebooks small footprint PCs (such as those with a Mini-ITX motherboard), high-end upgradable Office Printers, and networking hardware like routers.

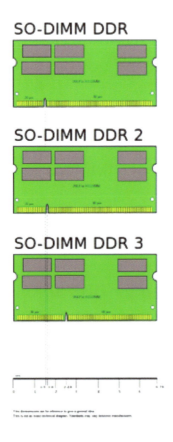

RAM DDR TYPES

RAM Generations

Besides the different sizes of RAM (DIMM and SO-DIMM) each has different generations – the most common now are DDR (1), DDR2 and DDR3. DDR stands for (Double Data Rate), with the number following simply being the generation; that is to say,
DDR2 replaced DDR as the standard type of memory around 2004. DDR3 became the most common type of memory for new computers in late 2009.

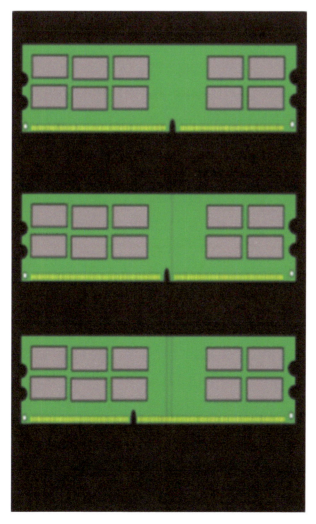

Each generation of DDR runs at different voltages and significantly different speeds; newer kinds of RAM are not backwards compatible (you cannot use older generations of DDR in newer motherboards).

RAM

RAM (Random Access Memory, referred to by retailers as just (memory), is similar to the short term memory of the computer.

Things the computer accesses regularly (like frequently used program files) or needs to store temporarily (like something you cut or copy to the clipboard in the operating system to paste somewhere else) are stored in RAM.

The RAM used by the vast majority of computers today is SDRAM (Synchronous Dynamic Random Access Memory). This means is that the RAM carries out instructions in sync with the CPU, and isn't something which you'll need to recall often.

RAM is referred to as random access because anything stored in RAM can be accessed in the same amount of time, regardless of where it's stored on the module.

This is different to the way a hard drive works, which uses physical parts that need to move to the correct place to access data.

Since it does not have to wait for physical parts to find the data, RAM is much faster than magnetic media (hard drives) and optical media (CD/DVD drives); however, the massive trade-off: RAM is an example of volatile memory.

This means that all the data stored in RAM is lost when the computer is turned off while data kept on a hard drive (which is a non-volatile form of storage) is kept safe and sound.

RAM

The other big difference between RAM and hard drives is the price to capacity ratio.
More RAM is better, there isn't much point in getting much more RAM than you need.
Most desktop motherboards have 4 memory slots, and for both DDR2 and DDR3 2GB sticks are currently the most economical size to buy.
It's not difficult to get 8GB of RAM in a desktop these days. Notebooks generally have 2 slots, so the economical max is 4GB (which many laptops ship with by default).
It really depends on the rest of your system; the specs of the other hardware in your computer, the operating system you're running and what you intend to use the computer for. Hardware-wise, it makes no sense to have 4GB of RAM if you're running an old Pentium 4 on Windows XP – sure, you'll have a lot of RAM, but performance is being held back by other components.
As a general guide OS wise (referring to Windows; if you're using Ubuntu chances are you already know enough about computers and Mac's they tend to work well with most amounts of RAM).
A guaranteed minimum for XP (particularly the latest versions) is 1GB; Windows Vista and 7 really should have a minimum of 2GB.
You can get away with less. XP can run alright with 512MB (0.5GB), and Vista and 7 can get away with 1GB, but in all cases you'll have less performance.
For general use 2GB is a great amount for XP and anywhere between 3-4GB for Vista and 7.

Of course, if you're planning on doing intensive work with your computer – video editing, Photoshop work, playing games and the like – you might want to consider adding more.

Right now, 4GB is the ideal and few people will benefit from using more.

Chapter7

STORAGE DEVICES

Hard-Drives

In a sense of understanding; the head would be like a Boeing 747 flying at 45 feet above the ground at over 30,000 mph plus and counting every single blade of grass.

As remarkable as this technology is, the magnetic hard drive is still based on moving parts.

These parts will inevitably wear out over time, eventually making it very, very difficult to retrieve the data.

The average desktop hard drive lasts for around 4 years and the average laptop drive, for 3 years.

Older drives typically connect to the motherboard with an IDE cable and receive power from the PSU (Power Supply) through a Molex Connector.

The newer drives instead use a SATA cable and are powered through a SATA power connector.

BRANDS

Like most kinds of components, hard drive manufacturers all have fierce loyalty and criticisms – the "best brand" and the brands to avoid constantly change depending on who you ask.

My preference: SEAGATE and SAMSUNG.

Other people will tell you the exact opposite.

No matter which brand you choose you'll almost certainly have no problems.

If the data on the hard drive is invaluable, you should be making backups, which will protect you if your hard drive fails.

Most people agree that drives from Maxtor and Hitachi are better off avoided.

Both of these companies are notorious for having big problems with their drives in past years.

While there's every chance that their reliability has significantly improved, many people will still refuse to buy a drive

Just as RAM is like the computer's short-term memory, storage devices act like the computer's long-term memory; unlike RAM, storage these types of hard drives don't lose data when they lose power.

The most common type of storage device is the: MAGNETIC HARD DRIVE. The other common types are of optical disks such as CDs and DVD's.

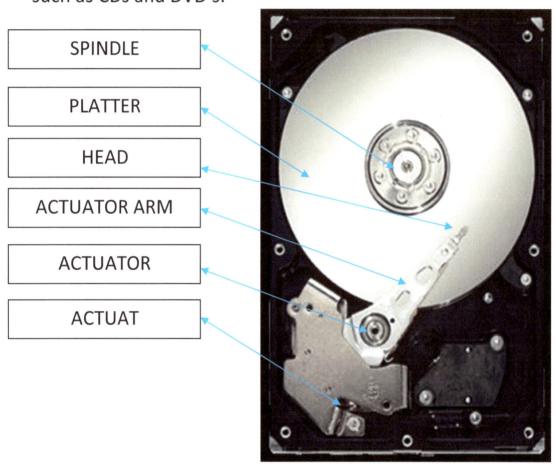

SPINDLE

PLATTER

HEAD

ACTUATOR ARM

ACTUATOR

ACTUAT

This is the most common storage device for computers! It offers great capacities for relatively low prices, and is generally very reliable and durable.

Hard drives like the one you'll find in your desktop today have been around since 1983; the smaller 2.5" drive you'll find in a laptop has been around since 1988.

The technology and scale used to make a magnetic hard drive work is impressive.

Simply, data is stored on platters, which are coated in a thin layer of magnetic material.

The platters are spun very fast on the spindle by a motor (most recent desktop hard drives rotate the platters 120 times every second!).

Another motor uses an actuator arm to move a device called the head back and forth over the platters.

Data is written to the platter by changing the magnetization of very small regions of the magnetic material.

Data is read by detecting the magnetization of the material in these regions which is then interpreted as binary data (either a 1 or a 0).

In general, laptops tend to use 5,400rpm drives while desktops tend to have 7200rpm drives.

It is not uncommon to find a 7,200rpm drive in a laptop when high performance is required and it is not uncommon for high-capacity drives used as extra storage to be running at 5,400rpm to save power and noise.

Laptop Internal Hard-drives

SOLID STATE DRIVES

SSDS

Solid State Drives are a relatively new arrival to mainstream computing but are already making big strides.
Instead of relying on platters and moving parts, SSDs rely on flash chips similar to the ones you'll find in USB memory
They perform much, much better than magnetic hard drives in a number of ways; there are no moving parts so they are silent, cool and more durable than a traditional hard drive.

Magnetic**H.D**.   Solid State **H.D.**

SOLID STATE HARD DRIVE

They use much less power and take very little time to start up.

They work in largely the same manner as RAM; it is possible to access files from multiple areas of the drive unlike magnetic drives which require the movement of the head to the area that needs to be read.

If you want an idea of the performance of an SSD, look up "SSD boot test" on YouTube – you'll see just how fast they are.

Multiple tests show the exact same computer booting in half the time with a SSD

This new technology is not cheap, and it is not without its problems.

A typical hard drive will give you around ($20 a GB).

You will easily spend much more on a higher performance SSD. This means that you either need lots of money for a big drive, or you need to have another conventional drive for the storage of most of your media.

Despite not having any moving parts, current SSDs have LIMITED LIFE-SPANS which are shorter than that of a conventional drive.

Newer SSDS have longer life-times, placing them in line with conventional drives.

Whether you should buy a SSD or not depends on a number of factors: your disposable income and how important performance and reliability all need to be taken into account.

It's difficult to recommend a SSD to a casual computer user; the added performance just isn't worth the extra cost unless you use your computer all the time.

Budget drives are becoming more commonplace, and the overall price to capacity ratio is falling rapidly.

On the other hand, if you use your computer all the time, performance is important to you and your drive's reliability is paramount, you may want to consider getting a SSD.

Capacity

It is important to get a hard drive with the right capacity.
In the vast majority of cases, a larger hard drive is better –
just because you only have a certain amount of data at the
moment doesn't mean that over time you won't need more.
On the other hand, if you've only got about 20GB of data at
the moment it makes little sense to buy a hard drive with 1TB
(or 1000GB) of storage.
Smaller capacity drives tend to be faster, make less noise and
use less power because they usually have fewer platters.
For a laptop, 160GB or 250GB is perfect. For a desktop, a
320GB drive is the biggest drive and is likely to be single-
platter.
If you need lots more storage and you have a laptop, you're
better off getting a high capacity external drive.

CPU Cache

Hard drives have something very similar.
It only has one level, and it isn't as fast as the CPU's cache,
but hard drives have a relatively small amount of storage for
data that is likely to be accessed regularly. In this case more
cache is better.
Most hard drives have 32MB of cache.
It is not necessary, but tries to get one of these if at all
possible.
If you get a drive with 8 or 16MB of cache, you'll find
performance isn't quite as smooth.

RPM - Drive Speed

The speed of a hard drive is very important, too.

Magnetic hard drives have two main speeds – 5,400rpm and 7,200rpm (although you can also buy 10,000rpm drives).

It's fairly obvious that a 7,200rpm hard drive will perform significantly better than a 5,400rpm drive.

There is a downside the trade-off for speed is higher power consumption, higher temperatures and more noise.

Chapter8

Optical Drives

Any device which can read optical discs (CDs, DVDs or the more recent HD-DVDs and Blu-Ray discs) is referred to as an optical drive.

Optical drives share data with the computer in the same way as hard drives; that is, they are connected to the motherboard either with an IDE cable or a SATA cable. They also use the same power connectors to receive power from the power supply; older drives using an IDE connector typically use the Molex Power Connector, newer drives with the SATA connector use the newer SATA power connector as well.

No matter what kind of disc the drive is reading or writing to, the process is practically identical.

When a disc is inserted into the drive it is rotated by a motor in a way which is somewhat similar to the spinning of a hard drive's platters.

A hard drive is designed to spin at a constant speed (measured in an optical drive, which is designed to spin a disc to achieve a constant data rate.

Optical Drives

As the circumference of the disc is higher towards the outside of the disc and the data must be read at a constant rate, a disc will spin slower when accessing data closer to the outside of the disc and faster when accessing data closer to the center.

Data is stored on a disc by pressing pits into a very thin reflective surface along a data path often referred to as the disc's groove.

A disc drive uses a LASER AND PHOTODIODES which detect light which travel along this groove (similar to the way a needle passes along a vinyl record).

When the laser travels over a pit the light is refracted differently to when the laser travels over the flat surface of the disc. This is detected by the photodiodes, which then output electrical signals that can be interpreted by the computer as data.

Writing to a disc is different. (Write Once Discs, like CD-Rs have a layer of organic dye as well as the reflective layer). Data is written to the disc with a much more powerful laser which is used to heat tiny sections of the dye, changing the reflectivity of the dye.

The heated areas cause differences in light refraction in the same way the pits of pressed CD's do.

Rewritable - Optical Drives

Rewritable discs like DVD-RWs work slightly differently again. Instead of using a layer of organic dye these use a phase-change layer.

These start off in a crystalline state which can then be changed to an amorphous state by heating with a more powerful laser.

Again, the amorphous sections of the disc act like the pits of a pressed disc.

Unlike the organic layer (CD-R) this change is reversible by reheating the amorphous sections, which causes them to revert to a crystalline state.

Brands

It's quite difficult to pick wrong with any manufacturer, but preferably optical drives by LG or Samsung.

You may come across a brand called Lite-On – these drives are manufactured by Sony, and also seem to be fairly reliable.

Floppy Drives

Once upon a time the storage a device of choice, floppy disks was popular from the mid-1970s until the late-1990s.

After being replaced by hard drives for the operating system, programs and data in the 80's, they continued to be used as portable storage.

Eventually they were superseded by USB Drives and CDs and DVDs.

It's unlikely that you'll find a floppy disk drive in any new computer – the reasoning is that if you really need access to one you can always purchase an external floppy disk drive that plugs into your computer via USB

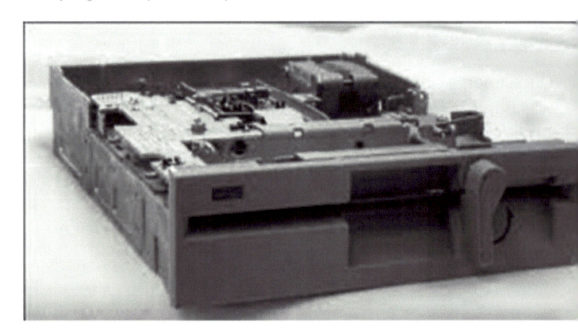

Chapter9

Power Connections

Remember the 20+4 Pin and 4+4 Pin connectors on the power supply?
This is where they go. The 4+4 pin socket is always right near the CPU socket (see below).
There are a few places where you may find the 20+4 Pin socket; it's right on the edge furthest from the back of the case, near the RAM slots.

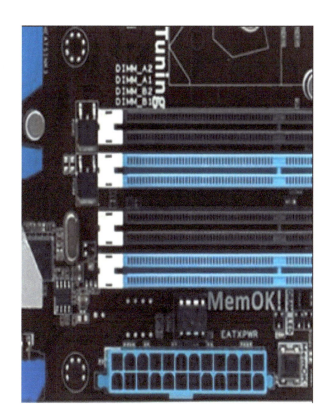

Chapter10

Expansion Slots

PCI

This is the most common slot for expansion cards. It has been superseded to an extent by the PCIExpress 1x slot, but many manufacturers still use the PCI slot for compatibility with older motherboards which don't have any PCI Express slots.

PCI EXPRESS (PCIE)

This is a new standard connector which has begun to slowly replace the PCI slot.
As you can see from the diagram above, it's available in a few different forms.
The most common one is the PCIE 16x slot, which replaced the AGP slot a few years ago.
The other common form is the PCIE 1x slot.
This is currently mainly used for network and sound cards, although the other standard expansion cards are beginning to become available on the PCIE interface.
Look at the example on the next page:

EXPANSION SLOTS

PCI -PCI Express 16x - 4x - 1x

One nice thing about the PCI Express slot is that any PCIE device can work in any PCIE slot as long as it fits.

For example, a graphics card with a PCIE 16x connecter can work in a 1x slot if you were to cut out the plastic back of the slot.
Likewise, a PCI Express 1x device will work perfectly in a 16x slot.
The only real difference between the slots is the number of lanes which the slot has, and therefore the amount of bandwidth between the device and the motherboard (that is, the amount of data which can be sent between the two at the same time).

Motherboard Cable Connections

FRONT PANEL AUDIO

FLOPPY DRIVE

FIRE WIRE

USB CONNECTIONS

FRONT PANEL

SATA

IDE

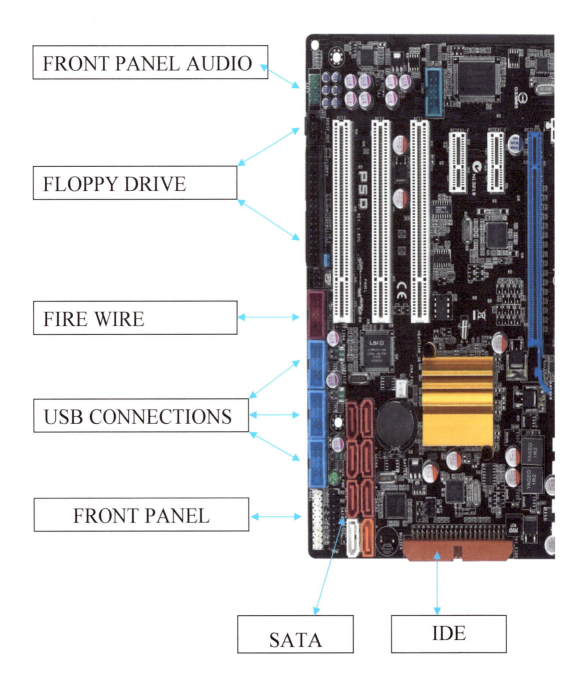

Chapter11

Audio Chipsets& Add-on Cards

In some computers, an audio chipset is a built-in part of the motherboard.
This happens most often in standard, pre-built computers without special audio hardware.
Having an onboard sound card can be beneficial because it takes up less space in a computer case than a separate sound card.

Motherboard Audio Chip

When it is time to replace or upgrade an onboard audio chipset that is part of a motherboard, the user leaves the original audio chipset in place and uses the software to disable it before installing a new upgraded sound card. Common manufacturers of audio chipsets include Advanced Micro Devices® (AMD), Sound-blaster®, Realtek® and Intel®.

PCI AUDIO CARDS

As you can see above audio or sound cards have options you must check to see what kind of usage or features you need.
Are you planning on expanding you home audio?
5.1 to 7.1 Surround?
Do you just need a good audio card for your computer desktop speakers?
2.1?

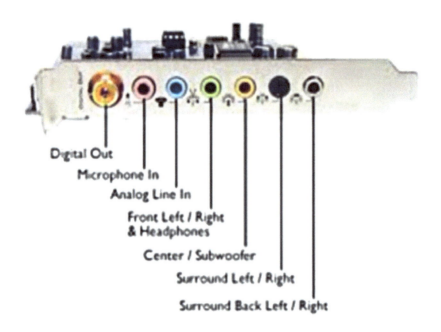

Digital Out

Microphone In

Analog Line In

Front Left / Right
& Headphones

Center / Subwoofer

Surround Left / Right

Surround Back Left / Right

Motherboard Audio

If you are into Music, Gaming or Home Theater then you will probably require a PCie type audio card. They also have many different options. Provided your computer is capable of supporting this particular configuration. Pricing is a major consideration based on what your computer can efficiently handle.

Dedicated sound cards have a number of improved or added features, which in turn produce better sound quality all around.

Features like higher signal-to-noise ratios, lower harmonic distortion, 24-bit sample rates, 192-kHz resolutions and of course additional APIs.

These additional features are what truly make a dedicated sound card worth the time and money it costs to install them and set them up to work properly.

One thing to keep in mind is that you will need a good set of speakers or a nice headset to truly hear the difference.

PCIE Audio Cards

CHAPTER 12

Externally Connected Devices

In general, USB devices are hot-swappable, which means that they can be unplugged and plugged into any USB slot at any time and will usually be recognized by the computer quickly. The other major advantage is that USB slots are so common – most computers now will have at least four to six USB ports, with new ones often having support for twelve or fourteen ports.

Front Case Connections

Front Panel

This is a series of pins which you use to connect the various parts of the front panel:
The power and reset buttons, the power and HDD LEDs and the chassis speaker (for those beeps that you may hear when you turn your computer on, for example).
However, for connecting the USB ports or similar ports to the motherboard – they have their own connectors.

Chapter13

Motherboard to Hardware Connections

IDE Parallel Cable

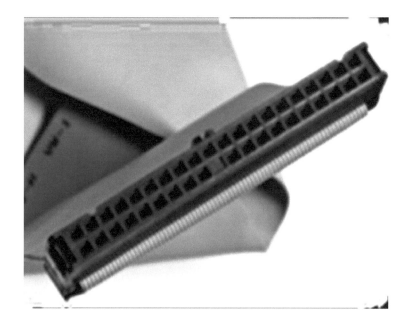

This was the connector of choice for connecting hard drives and optical drives until the introduction of SATA connectors in the example picture the connector has been placed at a 90° angle to make cables easier to manage.

Each IDE connector (or channel) was able to support "daisy-chaining", which is basically jargon for being able to connect two devices using a single IDE cable and connector.

For this to work, one device needed to be assigned as master, the other as a slave device, which basically decides which device appears to the computer first.

As IDE devices become less common (and less relevant) the connector will also eventually become less common on motherboards, similar to the floppy connector (more on that later). There are already some motherboards which do not have any IDE connectors.

SATA

This was introduced in 2003 and eventually replaced the IDE port as the standard connector for first hard drives and then optical drives.

Unlike IDE connectors each SATA port can only accommodate one device, but it has other advantages; it is much faster, for one (most SATA connectors today are able to transfer 3 gigabits/second, or 3000 megabits/second, while the latest IDE connector could only handle 133 megabits/second), the cables are much thinner and more manageable.

SATA also has the benefit of being hot-swappable; that is, it is possible to disconnect a SATA device and connect a different

SATA device using the same cable while the computer is still switched on (although it's often the case that you would have to manually rescan for it in the operating system).
IDE devices on the other hand need to be plugged in before the computer switched on.

USB

These connectors are used to add extra external USB ports (such as USB ports on the front panel of the PC), or to connect internal USB devices (such as internal card readers). Each connector supports either two USB ports or a single device. Most new motherboards have at least two internal USB headers (connectors), with some having as many as four.

Fire Wire

Even though a motherboard may not have a FireWire port on its I/O (Input/Output) panel, it does not mean that it does not have FireWire.

Many recent motherboards have at least one FireWire 400 header (FireWire 400 being the most common FW connector).

Unlike USB headers, each FireWire header can only support one FireWire port.

Floppy

The floppy connector is for connecting a floppy disk drive. The floppy power connector has been repurposed for card readers.

This motherboard connector has not been so lucky – it does not provide enough bandwidth for modern usage.
As very few people still use floppy disks most modern motherboards no longer have a floppy connector at all.

Front Panel Audio

This is the header to connect the microphone and headphone jacks on the front panel of your PC to the motherboard.
Most cases have two audio connectors inline on the same cable, AC97 and the other as HD AUDIO.
Both will fit on the same header on the motherboard, but only one will work.
Generally speaking, older motherboards will only support AC97 while newer motherboards will support both. It will usually say on the motherboard next to the header.

Chapter14

External Connections

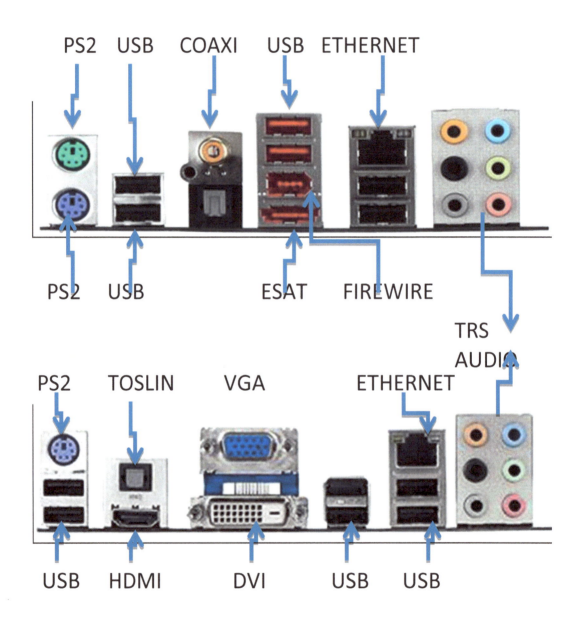

PS/2 Connectors

Before the introduction and widespread use of USB ports, PS/2 was the standard connector for mice and keyboards.

Their major advantage is guaranteed compatibility with older (and most new) hardware, particularly where there is only partial USB support.

This is because PS/2 devices are reported to the computer as soon as the computer starts up, which is not always the case with USB devices.

However, this comes with a major caveat – the devices must be plugged into the computer before it is turned on otherwise they are not recognized and will not work.

As PS/2 devices become less common in the face of new USB ones, it becomes very rare to see two PS/2 ports on the I/O panel.

However, most manufacturers leave one either just for the keyboard or a hybrid port which can take either a keyboard or a mouse.

This aids in situations where a USB device may not be recognized for various reasons, or if all other USB ports are used by non-PS/2 devices.

USB Ports

These ports are mostly used for everything now – they do not call it the Universal Serial Bus for nothing!

USB was designed to standardize the connection of computer peripherals (including keyboards, pointing devices, digital cameras, printers, portable media players, disk drives and network adapters, both to communicate and to supply electric power.

It has become commonplace on other devices, such as smart phones, PDAs and video game consoles.

USB has effectively replaced a variety of earlier interfaces, such as serial and parallel ports, as well as separate power chargers for portable devices.

USB-A

USB-A, Flash Drive for portable storage

USB-A, Standard Connection, "keyboard, mouse".

USB-B

The B-style connector is designed for use on USB peripheral devices.

The B-style interface is block shape, and has slightly beveled corners on the top ends of the connector.

Like the A connector, it uses the friction of the connector body to stay in place. The B-socket is an "upstream" connector that is only used on peripheral devices. Typically used for connection of a printer to your computer.

The B-socket is an "upstream" connector that is only used on peripheral devices. Typically used for connection of a printer to your computer.

MICRO-USB A

Recognized by the USB-IF, this connector can be found on newer mobile devices such as cell phones, GPS units, PDAs and digital cameras.

Micro-USB A offers a connection physically smaller in size to a USB Mini-b, while still supporting the high speed transfer rate of 480 Mbps and On-The-Go features.
The connection can be easily identified by its white-colored receptacle and compact 5 pin design.

Micro-USB A offers a connection physically smaller in size to a USB Mini-b, while still supporting the high speed transfer rate of 480 Mbps and On-The-Go features.
The connection can be easily identified by its white-colored receptacle and compact 5 pin design.

Micro-USB B

Designed exclusively for USB On-The-Go devices, this versatile connector can accept either a Micro-USB A or Micro-USB B cable connection.

This interface can be easily identified by its gray-colored receptacle and compact 5 pin design.
This connector type only exists as a receptacle for On-The-Go devices and will not exist on a cable.

USB Mini-B (5-Pin)

One drawback to the B-style connector is its size, which measures almost a half inch on each side.
This made the B-style interface unsuitable for many compact personal electronic devices such as PDAs, digital cameras, and cell phones.

As a result, many device manufacturers began the miniaturization of USB connectors with this Mini-b.
This 5-pin Mini-b is the most popular style of Mini-b connector, and the only one recognized by the USB-IF. By default, a Mini-b cable is presumed to have 5 pins.
This connector is quite small, about two-thirds the width of an A-style connector.
It is also specified for use in the newer standard called USB On-The-Go which allows peripheral devices to communicate with the presence of a host controller.

USB Mini-B (4-Pin)

Instead of the typical 5-pin Mini-b, this unofficial connector is found on many digital cameras, especially certain Kodak® models.

It resembles the shape of a standard B-style connector, with beveled corners; however it is much smaller in size.

It resembles the shape of a standard B-style connector, with beveled corners; however it is much smaller in size.

USB 3.0 "A" TYPE

Known as "Super Speed", this A-style connector is commonly found on host controllers in computers and hubs, the A-style connector is a flat, rectangular interface.
This interface holds the connection in place by friction which makes it very easy for users to connect and disconnect.
 Instead of round pins, the connector uses flat contacts which can withstand continuous attachment and removal very well.

The A-socket connector provides a "downstream" connection that is intended for use solely on host controllers and hubs. This connector is similar in size and shape to the A-Type connector used in USB 2.0 & USB 1.1 applications.
However, the USB 3.0 A-type has additional pins that are not found in the USB 2.0 & USB 1.1 A-Type.
The USB 3.0 connector is designed for USB Super Speed applications; however, it will carry data from slower speed connections, and it is backwards compatible with USB 2.0 ports. USB 3.0 "A" connectors are often blue in color to help identify them from previous versions.

USB 3.0 B-Type

The USB 3.0 B-Type connector is found on USB 3.0 devices. This connector is designed to carry data and power in USB Super Speed applications.

Cables with this connector are not backwards compatible with USB 2.0 or USB 1.1 devices; however USB 3.0 devices with this connection type can accept previous USB 2.0 and 1.1 cabling.

USB 3.0 MICRO-B

The USB 3.0 Micro B connector is found on USB 3.0 devices. This connector is designed to carry data and power in USB Super Speed applications.
Cables with this connector are not backwards compatible with USB 2.0 or USB 1.1 devices.

Cables with this connector are not backwards compatible with USB 2.0 or USB 1.1 devices.

Audio Connectors

These are what you use to connect or speakers or sound system to your computer. There are three main types of audio connectors:

TRS (analogue)

You will have almost certainly seen these ports before – they are the same sockets that you will find on an MP3 player like an iPod, or an older player like a Sony Discman.
In fact, you can easily plug headphones into the green port.
TRS stands for Tip, Ring, Sleeve, which is the design of a standard jack connector:

TIP-RINGSLEEVE

Most TRS sockets on a motherboard I/O panel will support 8 output channels:

· The Green Socket:

supports stereo output for two front speakers (or headphones)

· The Black Socket:

supports stereo output for two rear speakers

· The Grey Socket:

supports stereo output for two side speakers

· The Yellow Socket:

supports dual output for a center speaker and a subwoofer

*Also having 8 Output Channels and support 2 Input Channels:

· The Blue Socket:

supports stereo input for line in

· The Pink Socket:

supports "mono or stereo" microphone input

*Some older or cheaper motherboards only have the green, blue and pink sockets.

TOSLINK (DIGITAL/OPTICAL)

This connector is mainly for connecting a "Home Theatre Sound System" to your computer.
 It uses "Optical Fiber" to send large amounts of data through a single cable.

COAXIAL (DIGITAL)

This is similar to the TOSLINK Connector, but it relies on alternating electrical current to transfer data as opposed to the rapid blinking of light. They are both used for the same application, so it depends on what connector your speaker system has.

3.5 MM AUDIO

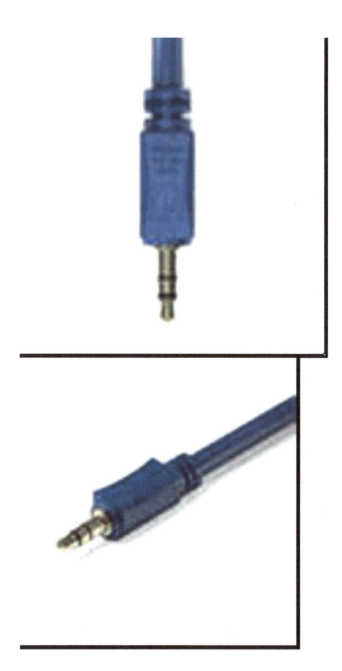

The 3.5 mm connector is commonly called a 1/8-inch connector or a mini-plug.

This connector is a small, thin metal plug that can be used to carry one, two, or even three signals.

The tip of the plug is separated from the sleeve of the connector by a concentric band of insulating material. For stereo or audio/video versions of the plug, there may be one or two additional metal bands, called rings, placed between the tip and the sleeve.

 3.5mm connectors are commonly used for computers and portable devices for mono or stereo audio. A computer's sound card uses these connectors for speakers, line-in/line-out connections, and also for microphones.

3.5MM OPTICAL MINI PLUG

Similar in size to the standard 3.5 mm connector, the 3.5 mm Optical Mini Plug is designed for digital audio application. This connector is commonly found on Apple® computers and some portable audio devices.
This type of connector is often adapted to a standard TOSLINK® connector

BANANA PLUGS

Banana plugs are often used to make speaker wire connections on amplifiers, speakers, and audio wall plates.
A banana plug has a metal pin that "bows" out in the middle, resembling the shape of a banana.
Banana plugs are normally used in pairs and mate with binding posts, which are typically found on higher-end amps and speakers.

RCA

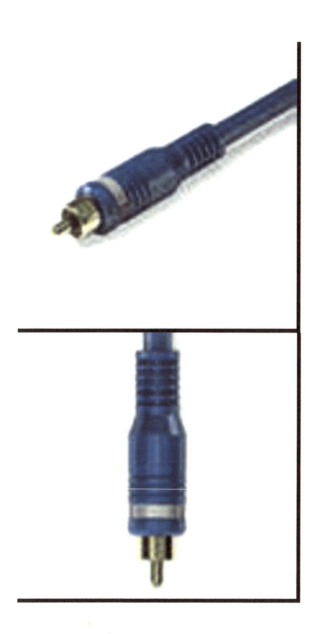

The RCA connector is used in several audio applications. S/PDIF (Sony®/Philips Digital Interface) is the "red book" standard for digital audio signal transfer.

For dual channel stereo audio, two RCA connectors deliver the analog composite audio signal to the left and right channels of audio.

In home theater, RCA is used as a powered subwoofer connection.

TOSLINK®

TOSLINK is the name of an optical interface for digital audio signals.

The TOSLINK (also known as EIAJ optical) connector is a small, round optical conductor housed in a square connector body. Originally intended for use solely with Toshiba CD players, it has been adopted by many other manufacturers and is standard equipment on many A/V sources, receivers and surrounds sound equipment.

Even though TOSLINK uses fiber optic cable, it is limited to a maximum cable length of about 5 meters, due to the low power of the LEDs used in transceivers.

Chapter15

GRAPHICS/VIDEO CARDS

PCI

Typical PCI cards used in PCs include: network cards, sound cards, modems, extra ports such as USB or serial, TV tuner cards and disk controllers. PCI video cards replaced ISA and VESA cards, until growing bandwidth requirements outgrew the capabilities of PCI; the preferred interface for video cards became AGP, and then PCI Express. PCI video cards remain available for use with old PCs without AGP or PCI Express slots. Three 5-volt, 32-bit, PCI expansion slots on an older motherboard.

PCIe

PCI Express: is a point-to-point connection, which means it does not share bandwidth but communicates directly with devices via a switch that directs data flow.
This allows for "hot swapping" or "hot plugging," which means cards in PCie slots can be changed without shutting

down the computer, and they consume less power than previous PCI technology.

PCIe

Interface (Bus) Type
PCI Express 3.0

Types of PCIe Formats

The initial rollout of PCI Express provided three consumer options: x1, x2, and x16.
These numbers represents the "lanes:" x1 has 1 lane; x2 has 2 lanes, and x16 has 16.
Each lane is bi-directional and consists of 4 pins.
Lanes in PCIe version 1.x had a lower delivery transfer rate, but PCIe 3.0 introduced a transfer rate of 500 megabytes per second (MBps) in each direction for a total of 1,000 MBps, or 1 gigabyte per second (GBps), per lane.

PCIe	Lanes	Pins	MBps	Purpose
x1	1	4	1 GBps	Device
x2	2	8	2 GBps	Device
x16	16	64	16 GBps	Graphics Card

PCIe and Graphics Cards

The 16-lane (x16) slot has replaced the Accelerated Graphics Port (AGP) on many motherboards and fits a PCIe graphics card.
Boards that include the x1 and x2 slots usually have them for other components, such as sound or networking cards.

As computer graphics demands increase, x32 and x64 slots may become available, and future versions of PCIe might improve upon lane data rates.

Nvidia Geforce 2GB Pci-e X16 Single Slot Hdmi+DVI Gaming HD Video

This video card like the one below runs around $ 80.00

Suitable for the average user which like to play games

Chapter 16

ADD-ON CARDS

EXTRA I/O (USB, FIREWIRE)

New motherboards support 12 USB ports and 2 FireWire ports, but you can never have too many! Besides, you may want to breathe some life back into an older computer that was around before (USB 2 or USB 1,). These PCI cards will give you all the ports you need.

Storage Controllers

Perhaps it's time to give your old faithful computer an upgrade– maybe it's time to get one of those new SATA hard drive But, you don't have any SATA ports!
It'll get you the ports you need; IDE, SATA or eSATA.
You will now be able to connect that new hard drive or optical drive.

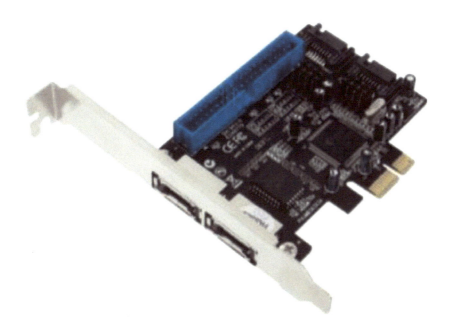

TV Tuners

One thing lot of people overlook is that their PC can make a great Digital Video Recorder (DVR).
Get a TV tuner card into your PC and you'll be recording video from the TV in no time.
Dual tuners even let you watch something while recording something else at the same time.

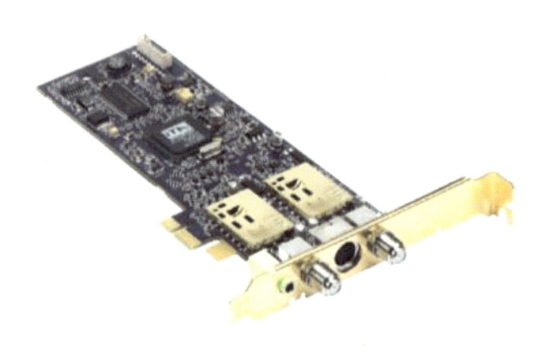

Computer Fundamentals for Adults

The Case and Components

BOOK 2

Computer Fundamentals for Adults

Home & Home Office Networking
&
"Spyware and Viruses"

www.ingramcontent.com/pod-product-compliance
Lightning Source LLC
Chambersburg PA
CBHW041427050326

40689CB00003B/684